THE
Archive Photographs
SERIES

SAUNDERSFOOT
AND TENBY

Best Wishes

D. Ken Daniels.

Unofficial Arms of Saundersfoot.

The unofficial Arms of Saundersfoot. The original Arms was designed by Mr Fred Pulford in 1912 for Mr Thomas Owen (Thos Owen) who kept the Fancy Bazaar in Railway Street. The crested ware that was sold in the shop was produced by W.H. Goss, Falcon Works, Stoke-on-Trent. An enamel Goss sign displayed outside the Fancy Bazaar declared: "Goss ware sold here".

Front-cover illustration: A large crowd of local people gathered for the 1927 Mayor's Sunday civic service and parade through the streets of Tenby. Margaret Jane Jenkins was installed as the town's first citizen.

THE
Archive Photographs
SERIES

SAUNDERSFOOT AND TENBY

Compiled by
D. Ken Daniels

CHALFORD

First published 1995
Copyright © D. Ken Daniels, 1995

The Chalford Publishing Company
St Mary's Mill, Chalford,
Stroud, Gloucestershire, GL6 8NX

ISBN 0 7524 0192

Typesetting and origination by
The Chalford Publishing Company
Printed in Great Britain by
Redwood Books, Trowbridge

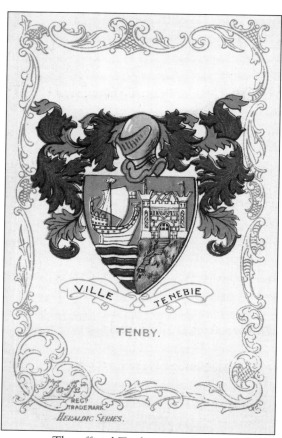

The official Tenby coat of arms.

Contents

Foreword

By Councillor Mrs Rosemary Hayes, J.P., Chairman of Saundersfoot Community Council, 1995–6

I am very honoured to be asked by a friend of very long standing to write an introduction to this excellent new publication. Most of us have photographs and postcards not only from our own childhood but also from many years before. Sadly, many of these tend to get lost or mislaid and I, therefore, congratulate Ken's initiative in producing this memorable book so that these pictorial records are available for generations to come. The selected images reveal a wealth of information and will be, I feel sure, of great interest to very many people.

Saundersfoot has a very interesting history. The earliest record of local government was the formation of the parish council in 1894 with members meeting at first in the schoolroom of St Issell's church. This schoolroom was built in the 1820s and until 1870 it was the only school in the area. The building, which was recently renovated, is still used today for Sunday School and for other functions. Saundersfoot also has a proud industrial past with its iron ore and brickworks and the Bonville's Court Colliery from which some of the finest anthracite in the world was extracted. This was exported to many countries, its most famous customer being Queen Victoria who insisted that it be used on the Royal Yacht because of its smokeless qualities.

The dominant present-day industry is tourism which began to develop in Saundersfoot at the end of the last century. Like the oak tree it has grown remarkably from small beginnings. Over the last hundred years thousands upon thousands of visitors have been charmed and entertained by the village, the most important of whom were surely those soldiers who stormed our beaches in rehearsals for the D Day landings of 1944.

Tenby, meanwhile, has its own long and rich maritime history. Smugglers used this coast as well as the more reputable merchants whose cargo vessels once packed the superb harbour. A lifeboat has been *in situ* since the nineteenth century and its crews, over the years, have received many silver and bronze medals. St Margaret's Fair, granted by Royal Charter in Elizabethan times, is also among the events and institutions which have shaped the character of this delightful town as, too, is the much loved grammar school, the author and myself being among the hundreds of pupils educated there. It is now a further education centre and library.

I hope, dear reader, that when reading this book you will very much enjoy your historical tour through Saundersfoot and Tenby.

Rosemary Hayes, J.P.

Mr & Mrs Roger Griffiths and family (Mary and Blodwen) outside the Cash Stores, Railway Street, Saundersfoot, 1910.

Introduction

This book has been published as a result of repeated requests from local inhabitants in the two communities of Saundersfoot and Tenby. Most of the pictorial content consists of a wide variety of postcards and photographs taken from my personal collection built up over more than forty years. Together, these images attempt a thorough review of streets, social events, changing scenes and personalities in these two neighbouring areas. Although carefully captioned the book does not feature an extensive array of facts as these have already been researched and recorded by other authors and historians.

Both Saundersfoot and Tenby were never without discerning admirers as fashionable seaside resorts during the Victorian and Edwardian period. Today, their popularity is still evident with large numbers of visitors attracted each year to this charming historical area of Pembrokeshire.

Railway Street, Saundersfoot, *c.* 1920.

The importance of their past development and natural beauty was well-recorded and highlighted through the camera's eye by Charles Smith Allen, his two sons, H. Mortimer Allen and Samuel J. Allen and by Arthur Squibbs. We must be extremely grateful to these photographic artists for leaving us such a rich pictorial legacy for both Saundersfoot and Tenby.

The artist, Augustus John, closely connected with Tenby, surely voiced the thoughts of many present-day visitors to the area when he said: "you may travel the world over, but you will find nothing more beautiful; it is so restful, so colourful and so unspoilt." These words echo also my sentiments for Saundersfoot and Tenby's fascinating past in pictures.

D. Ken Daniels

D. Ken Daniels
May 1995

One
Saundersfoot:
St Bride's, Milford
Terrace, High Street,
Cambrian Terrace

Rushy Lake, c. 1928.

Rhodewood Terrace, *c.* 1904. Richard Norris' daughter, Mrs Sarah Taylor lived in the big house of Rhodewood Lodge, also referred to as the "Turkish House".

St Bride's, *c.* 1920.

St Bride's at the junction of Sandyhill Road, *c*. 1906.

The Glen and St Bride's Hill, *c*. 1908. In the 1920s the occupants of the houses were: No 1 – Mr & Mrs Copland (daughter, Mrs Usher), No 2 – Mr & Mrs Picton, No 3 – Major & Mrs Silverthorne (the major always carried his army "adder stick" especially on his cliff walks to Monkstone), No 4 – Mr & Mrs Esnof, owners of two large great danes whose barking could be heard far and wide.

The Glen, *c.* 1934.

Swallow Tree Woods, *c.* 1913. The beautiful lady featured was Mr Thomas Owen's daughter, Nan.

Harbour and village viewed from Swallow Tree Woods, *c*. 1909.

The anticline of Ladie's Cave, the Glen and Back Beach, *c*. 1908.

Carrington Hotel, *c.* 1930. Now known as the St Bride's Hotel it possesses a superb view of the village. Both hotels had their own postcards printed for advertising purposes.

St Bride's rock garden, *c.* 1938.

Panoramic view of Saundersfoot, *c.* 1905, showing the railway, St Issell's House, Bonville's Court colliery office and the Evelyn Coffee Tavern.

The back entrance to St Issell's House (known by locals as the "big house") as seen from St Bride's Hill, *c.* 1907.

Saundersfoot, c. 1901. Besides some notable buildings the picture also shows "Planks Corner" and features, on the right, Mr Morgan Howells, a local timber carter loading wood imported

from Ireland. This image was sold as a giant postcard by Thomas Owen of the Fancy Bazaar, Saundersfoot.

General view of the village from Ragged Staff, *c*. 1932.

Milford Terrace, *c*. 1910 showing Dr Stewart Jones' chauffeur and the Gower House. This was a children's home which closed after the Second World War.

Milford Terrace, *c.* 1910. The annual Studt's Fair was held on the area of ground in front of the wall known as the "Paddock". This was later replaced by Danter's Fair which set up by the harbour.

Milford Terrace, *c.* 1927. The gentleman under the large copper beech on the right is William Beddoe of Cambrian House (Billy Beddoe's butcher shop). In May 1969 his name was preserved for posterity in Beddoe's Court, which is situated at the junction of Brewery Terrace and Milford Terrace.

High Street, c. 1921.

High Street, c. 1912. The pavement on the right was made of beach pebbles laid on their sides. Adjacent to the Thomas Memorial Chapel is Myrtle Cottage. In 1880 this was the first post office in the village. There was initially no delivery of letters so if a letter was received by the staff it was placed in the window to be personally collected. In 1887 the post office was moved to Woodbine Cottage and in 1892 it moved again to 1 Railway Street. Later, it moved back to the High Street. The present-day post office is situated in Brewery Terrace.

High Street, *c*. 1908. On the right is the Thomas Memorial Chapel and manse, Rose Cottage and Norland House. The wall of the latter house was built from Templeton bricks with iron railings forged at Tom David's Woodside foundry.

Hean Castle, *c*. 1905. It was formerly known as the "Picton Castle Inn".

Cambrian Terrace, *c.* 1905. The crossroads area is known as "Cole's Corner". St Issell's House is in the background.

Cambrian Terrace, *c.* 1903.

Cambrian Terrace, *c.* 1922. Bonville's Court colliery office is on the left.

Cambrian Terrace, *c.* 1920, showing Johnnie Ormond's omnibus outside the hotel.

Cambrian Terrace, *c.* 1932. The pictured bus was part of the local Green's service to Tenby, Narberth and Haverfordwest.

CAMBRIAN STREET, SAUNDERSFOOT

Willing locals pose for the photographer, Cambrian Terrace, *c.* 1903.

Two

The Harbour

The harbour, c. 1875. Built in 1829 from local and imported stone Saundersfoot became a busy and important harbour exporting the hard glassy anthracite from Bonville's Court Colliery which was opened in 1842. Large quantities of this coal were exported to Kent (to fuel the malting process), to Ireland, and to Cornwall where it enabled the smelting of tin from the Cornish mines. Many local boats and schooners brought back on their return to Saundersfoot such cargoes as grain, flour, sugar, tea, soap, beer and other grocery sundries. Well-known local sea captains and their vessels from this period of boom include the *Pride of Wales* captained by Pierce Bennett of 3 Railway Street; the *Verbena* of Captain Graham who lived in Cambrian Terrace, Captain Derby's *Woodcock* (he lived in High Street) and the *Lady of the Isles* skippered by Captain Jack Davies of Brewery Stores.

The harbour, *c.* 1903.

The unloading side of the harbour, *c.* 1905. Assistance for unloading cargoes was given by the steam crane operated for many years by Ben Lewis.

The harbour, *c.* 1931, showing a steam-driven vessel berthed at a coal loading chute.

Local sailing and rowing boats at their moorings in Saundersfoot harbour, *c.* 1927.

The harbour, *c.* 1905. Note the anthracite coal drams on the harbour railway line, the blacksmith's shop and the weighbridge.

Jack Childs, the Saundersfoot harbour pilot making his way to the shore, *c.* 1922.

"Childs' corner", Saundersfoot harbour, *c.* 1911. This mooring area of the harbour was named after Jack Childs who long kept his sailing and rowing boats there.

A large gathering watches a loaded coastal vessel leaving Saundersfoot harbour, *c.* 1930.

29

Saundersfoot, Harbour and Village.

The harbour, *c*. 1907. The small inner harbour adjacent to the basin walls was used as a dry dock for yacht repairs.

The harbour, *c*. 1926. Seawater was retained by the manually operated sluice gates. These were opened at low water to clear the harbour mouth sandbank. The released seawater also assisted in keeping the harbour free of coal dust silt.

The harbour, *c.* 1928. The two yachts, *Ranee* and the *Otter* belonged to Charles Vickerman and Dr D. Pennant.

The harbour, *c.* 1909, showing the unloading steam crane.

The harbour and Front Beach during the annual winter storms, *c.* 1919.

The Pitchings (so called because its foundations were set in pitch) and the breakwater, *c.* 1922.

Longshore sports and regatta in the harbour, c. 1908. The sports consisted of swimming, diving, rowing, obstacle and barrel races. The most entertaining event was surely "walking the greasy pole" in which competitors had to touch the Union Jack at its end.

A regatta in progress at Saundersfoot harbour, c. 1931.

Captain Pierce Bennett's *Pride of Wales* waiting to enter the harbour, *c.* 1919.

Saundersfoot Railway with the weighbridge (now Saundersfoot Yacht Club) and the blacksmith's shop, *c.* 1910.

Anthracite coal drams and loading chutes, *c*. 1922.

The village green, *c*. 1904.

The harbour in 1947 showing the annual Danters fair on the village green.

Danters fair at Saundersfoot, 1940s. On the left is the concrete base of the NAAFI canteen building. This caught fire and burnt to the ground on 10 July 1941.

Bonville's Court colliery office, *c.* 1903 with, in front, the railway loop line to the unloading stage, *c.* 1903.

Following a disastrous fire in 1913 the Bonville's Court colliery office was gutted destroying the colliery records. The reconstructed building now houses the tourist information centre.

The harbour viewed from entrance No 2, *c.* 1930.

Saundersfoot Railway loop section which ran from the harbour to the incline plane, *c.* 1924.

Three

Railway Street
(now the Strand),
Coppet Hall, St Issell's

Railway Street, *c.* 1909. The post office moved to 1 Railway Street in 1892.

The *Rosalind* steams into Railway Street on her return to Stepaside, *c.* 1901. The boy on the right is about to fill a container from the water point behind him.

Railway Street, *c.* 1900. The anthracite coal drams drawn by the *Rosalind* travelled from Stepaside to the harbour and the waiting ships. The gentleman in the white apron standing outside his Fancy Bazaar shop is Thomas Owen (known locally as "Thos" Owen, see p. 62).

Front Beach, *c.* 1900, showing carters transporting shingle from the beach for use later as a building material.

Peace Day party for the residents of Railway Street, Front Beach, 1918.

Railway Street, *c.* 1912, showing the *Rosalind* approaching the Globe Inn on her return journey to Stepaside.

The *Rosalind* returning to Stepaside after the end of the miners' day shift, Railway Street, *c.* 1923.

Craig-y-Mor or Rock Villa at the end of Railway Street, *c.* 1920.

Front Beach, viewed from Craig-y-Mor and the boathouse, *c.* 1900. Wren Cottage and Penrose can be seen further along the sands.

Coppet Hall, *c*. 1913. The lady resting by the Friars Brook post is Nan Owen (see also p. 12)

Coppet Hall, *c*. 1902. The Saundersfoot Railway reached Coppet Hall through the Railway Street tunnel and then via the short and long tunnels it arrived in Stepaside.

Coppet Hall caravan site, 1948.

Coppet Hall dunes showing the "changing" tents for bathers pitched amidst the sand and marram grass, *c.* 1924.

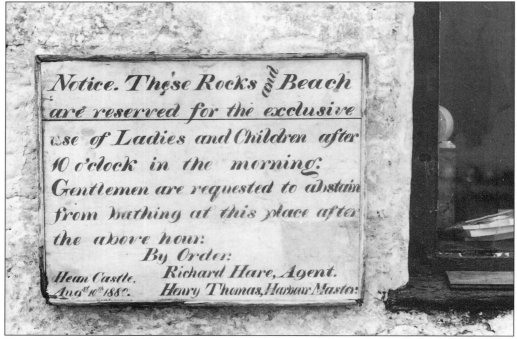

Hean Castle sign, dated 10 August 1880, requesting gentlemen to abstain from bathing after 10 a.m. on Coppet Hall beach. This notice is now in the possession of the author.

Coppet Hall, *c.* 1925. The Black Walk footpath commences here.

Black Walk, *c.* 1904. The black shale of the footpath meanders through the tree-lined meadow.

Black Walk, *c.* 1907. The footpath passes around the back of Marylands and the Old Mill.

The end of the Black Walk footpath at St Issell's Church, *c.* 1904.

Saundersfoot Church (dedicated to St Issell) and schoolroom, *c.* 1905. It is situated midway between the village and Hean Castle. The National School, built in the 1820s, was the first in the vicinity. The building has recently been tastefully restored.

Interior of St Issell's Church, *c*. 1910. In 1919 the pulpit was moved to the right hand side to accommodate a canopy and the 1914–18 roll of honour board.

Passengers waiting on the "down" platform for the Pembroke Dock train, Saundersfoot railway station, *c*. 1906. The gentleman with the Gladstone bag was the local Medical Officer, Dr William Clement Evans.

The "up" train to Whitland awaiting the "down" train to Pembroke Dock, Saundersfoot railway station, *c.* 1914. The station master is William Owen.

Bonville's Court Colliery, *c.* 1907. The colliery was opened in 1842 and provided excellent quality anthracite coal up until it closure in April 1930 after 88 years in production. During these years the coal industry was the mainstay of the local economy.

Woodside Foundry.

SAUNDERSFOOT, 8/r 27 1893

Memo. from **T. DAVID & CO.**

To Mr Griffiths — Tenby

Dear Sir

We are sorry to say that we have quite failed to make a Cog wheel by the old one neither had we a pattern that would suit.

You will however have no difficulty in getting it from the matter of the machine.

Give the no and mark

Describe it as follow

+ 26   Diameter 5 1/2" over

Pitch of teeth 5/8". Hole 1 1/8"

also no of teeth

Yours

TD

T. DAVID & CO.,

GENERAL FOUNDERS, IMPLEMENT AGENTS, MACHINISTS, HARDWARE DEALERS, &c.,

Telegrams—"FOUNDRY, SAUNDERSFOOT."

Note from Tom David & Co. to a Mr Griffiths of Tenby explaining that he was unable to make him a new cog wheel.

Woodside foundry and brickworks, c. 1922. The concern was operated in 1845 by Thomas Stokes and from 1850 by Messrs David and Parcell.

Saundersfoot.

Saundersfoot
seems to be unrivalled for those
in need of "Change."

How
they
say
Good-day
at
SAUNDERSFOOT

Four

Saundersfoot's
Social History

Mr & Mrs Roger Griffiths who were married in October 1900. They lived in London House, Railway Street where they opened a drapery business called the Cash Stores. Their advertisement in the *Narberth, Whitland and Clynderwen Weekly News* of Thursday 5 May 1910 states that "our Milliner has just returned from London with a large stock of the very latest in Ladies and Children's Trimmed and Untrimmed Black and Coloured Hats, Fancy Drapery of all descriptions. Prices low – quality right. Please call and inspect at Roger Griffiths's Cash Stores, Saundersfoot." Besides this venture Mr Griffiths also began a coal haulage business and was a most popular personality delivering coal in the locality.

Saundersfoot Improvements Committee carnival float (tennis theme), 1922.

St Issell's Church Youth XI, 1947/48. Standing: Graham Cole, Bryn Evans, Martin Palmer, Jeffrey Thomas, Ken Daniels, Robin Mosson, David Williams. Kneeling: Raymond Craig, David James, David Davies, John Lawrence.

John Edwards the water carrier. Water was carried to householders from any of the five street supply taps for ½d per journey.

Rev & Mrs Vaughan Thomas outside their house, "The Edgecombe" with a 1926 Morris Oxford. Mrs Plank's corner sweet shop is on the right. Rev Thomas was a Baptist minister.

Saundersfoot Ramblers concert party, 1914. From left to right, back row: Muriel Wright, Iris Phillips, -?-. Middle row: Majorie Howells, Maisie Beddoe, Annie Bennett, Mary Griffiths, Eva Bennett,. Front row: Nellie Thomas, Maisie Thomas.

Laying the foundation stone of the New Village Hall and Community Centre, 10 June 1960. From left to right: Jack Parcell, Capt Tom Stickings, Harold Davies, Major E. Molyneux, Rt. Hon. Lord Merthyr, Rev Glyn Evans, Rev Vaughan Thomas.

SAUNDERSFOOT VILLAGE HALL COMMITTEE

Programme

of the

Ceremonial Opening

of the

New Village Hall and Community Centre

(to be known as the Regency Hall)

by

Rt. Hon. LORD MERTHYR, D.L., T.D., J.P.

on

SATURDAY, JUNE 24th, 1961

AT 3 P.M.

Programme for the ceremonial opening of the New Village Hall and Community Centre, 24 June 1961.

SAUNDERSFOOT VILLAGE HALL COMMITTEE
(Opening Week June 24th - July 1st)

A Grand Opening Concert

at

THE REGENCY HALL

on

SATURDAY, 24th JUNE, 1961

given by

Morriston Orpheus Choir

President : J. T. MORGAN, Esq., Swansea

(Nine times First Prize Winners at Welsh National Eisteddfod)

B.B.C., I.T.V., Royal Albert Hall, Festival Hall, Kingsway Hall
and Provincial Concerts

ROYAL COMMAND PERFORMANCE, 1957

Founder Conductor : IVOR E. SIMS

Conductor :	**Accompanist :**
EURFRYN JOHN, A.R.C.O.	**D. J. REES, F.R.C.O.**

GUEST ARTISTES

FLORENCE POLSON-TAYLOR, *Soprano*

JONAH PHILLIPS, *Baritone*

President : Ald. HAYDEN WILLIAMS, J.P.

PROGRAMMES   -   -   6D. EACH

Printed by H. G. Walters (Publishers) Ltd., Tenby and Narberth.

Programme for the grand opening concert at The Regency Hall, 24 June 1961.

Class 5 at Saundersfoot Council School, 1906. On the left is the headmaster, Charles Phillip Turl who was also the organist at St Issell's Church.

Mr Thomas Owen of 8 Railway Street pictured here in 1893. Originally from Maenclochog and a watchmaker by trade Owen opened his shop in Railway Street and called it the Fancy Bazaar. Items sold included a wide range of children's toys, china, glass, jewellery and postcards. Many of his postcards are featured in this book.

Miss Maisie Beddoe, for many years an infant teacher at the Saundersfoot Ridgeway Road Council School.

Women's Institute Choir pictured in December 1969. Earlier that year in June they had been selected as one of two Pembrokeshire choirs to appear at the Royal Albert Hall. From left to right, back row: Rene John (soloist), Ivy Poole (Secretary), Doreen Phillips (soloist). Front row: Gwyneth Palmer (conductor), Mary Griffiths (pianist), Mrs Hobbs (deputy pianist)

Charlie Cox pictured in 1961. A master mason by trade he worked for Fred Richards the local building contractor. An excellent sportsman, he was a member of the powerful Saundersfoot Utd football XI in the 1920s, and a victorious competitor at each year's "greasy pole" event at the longshore sports. In latter years Charlie has been a popular leader of the New Year's Day charity swim.

Opening the new premises of the Saundersfoot branch of the British Legion, 9 March 1963. From left to right: Standard Bearer L. Davies, A. Lawrence, Dr T.R. Griffiths, C. Hitch, W.J. Cole, J. Parcell, V. Morris, T. Williams.

"SERVICE NOT SELF"

BRITISH LEGION
SAUNDERSFOOT BRANCH

•

OPENING

OF NEW BRANCH PREMISES

(ADJOINING REGENCY HALL, SAUNDERSFOOT)

on

Saturday, 9th March, 1963

at 6.15 p.m.

BY

Dr. T. R. GRIFFITHS,
Branch President.

•

OUR GRATEFUL THANKS TO YOU ALL
FOR YOUR HELP AND SUPPORT

HISTORY

In 1961 the Branch was under notice to quit its old premises, and experiencing considerable difficulty in finding alternative premises until the Village Hall Committee generously agreed to lease a part of the spare land at the rear of and adjoining the Regency Hall, provided the Branch could raise the money to build. Nineteen sixty-two was the 40th Anniversary of the Branch, and under the inspiration of its Chairman, Mr. Alwyn Griffiths, and the generosity of Mr. Aubrey Lawrence in volunteering to supervise any building activities, enthusiasm was aroused and an appeal launched in January, 1962. The response by friends and members was so heartening that the Committee decided to go ahead and build its own premises, and the foundations were started on 4th April. The diligent, hard and conscientious work of a small team of enthusiastic amateurs, under the skilful guidance of Mr. Aubrey Lawrence, succeeded in achieving the result which you are seeing tonight. The rooms are not quite complete, but are sufficiently so to enable the Branch to start its social activities once again. Below is a list of those who have given freely of their labour to make this possible; their sole reward being the satisfaction of seeing the rooms built, which it is hoped will be of benefit not only to the present members, but future generations.

Builder-in-Chief :

A. Lawrence ... ... 500 hrs.	T. Cordon ... ... 96 hrs.
A. G. Griffiths (Chairman) 496½ hrs.	Brian Waters ... ... 74 hrs.
J. Powell ... ... 341½ hrs.	Clifton John ... ... 55 hrs.
H. Phelps ... ... 292½ hrs.	J. Parcell (Hon. Treasurer) 34½ hrs.
C. Hitch (Hon. Secretary) 226 hrs.	J. Davies ... ... 32 hrs.
D. Poole ... ... 223½ hrs.	T. Williams ... ... 24½ hrs.
P. Meyler ... ... 169½ hrs.	L. Davies ... .:. ... 12 hrs.
T. O. Poole (The Bay) ... 120 hrs.	G. Poole ... ... 8½ hrs.
N. Evans ... ... 96 hrs.	S. Taverner ... ... 8 hrs.
	C. Richards ... ... 6½ hrs.

Less than 6 hours: C. Price, P. Flanighan, Alan Griffiths, B. Way.

Total : 2,848 man hours up to 31st January.

Special Help: Major E. Molyneux—plans; Miss M. Beddoe—Committee Room Table; Mr. Norman Evans—decor, and design and construction of Legion sign; Mr. Tom Roblin—papering rooms; Mr. Rowen—glazing windows; Mr. E. Thomas —carpets and making curtains; Mr. Vic Morris—gift of iron girder and free use of mechanical equipment; Mr. G. Neil—crane driver; Mr. Don Richards—acting storeman and tea-maker; Hon. T. O. Lewis—loan of mechanical aid and scaffolding; Mr. David Thomas—excavating; Mr. John Rees—free loan of concrete mixer; Mr. Ben Morris—assisting with plastering.

Western Telegraph, Haverfordwest

McLoughlin Brothers' corner shop, 1953. At that time it was one of three places in the village where petrol could be purchased. It is now a small supermarket.

"Willie" Burgess lived in Railway Street and was in the family bakery business as a master baker. He was Saundersfoot's harbour master from April 1963 until October 1983.

Miss Mary Griffiths, the talented musical teenager from London House, Railway Street.

Mary Griffiths was awarded the British Empire Medal in the 1983 Queen's birthday honours list. "Miss Music's" contribution to the local and national musical scene will long be remembered by many of her Pembrokeshire audiences.

St George's Day parade, 1964. From left to right: Ben Williams, Rev Glyn Evans, William Rogers, Gwyn Llewellyn, Tommy Williams, Don John, Trevor Poole and Stanley Harries.

Saundersfoot Women's Institute's performance of *Merry England* held in the Drill Hall, 1945. Among those pictured are Arthur Parcell, Joan Osbourne, Mrs Bennett, Maisie Beddoe, Muriel Lloyd, Mona Lawrence, Mrs Lewis, Jackie Parcell, Mrs Allen, Mrs Rogers, Mrs Parcell and Mrs Thomas.

The children of Saundersfoot at the Drill Hall during the Silver Jubilee celebrations for George V in 1935.

73

∴ **DRILL HALL, SAUNDERSFOOT.** ∴
(By permission of O.C. 425 Coast Regt. R.A., T.A.)

FIRST ANNUAL

EISTEDDFOD

(Sponsored by Amroth Seagulls Football Club)

will be held in the above Hall on

FRIDAY, OCTOBER 27th, 1950 at 5 p.m.

President : Ald. D. H. Pennant, D.S.O.

ADJUDICATORS.

Music : Mr. Clifford Goldstone, L.T.S.C., A.R.A.M. Carmarthen.
Literature : Miss Madge Thomson, A.L.A.M., M.R.S.T. S-foot.
Love Letter : Ald. D. H. Pennant, D.S.O.
Prize Bags : Miss Gwen Llewellyn, Stepaside.

Conductor : Mr. Stuart John.
Accompanists : Miss Mary Griffiths.
Miss Gwynneth Ellis, A.T.C.L.

Admission - Adults 3/6 and 2/6.   Children half price.

Programmes - 3d. each, post free 4d.

Joint Secretaries : Mr. R. Ellis, Sunnydale, Stepaside.
Mr. A. Aldgate, Hill House, Amroth.

Programme for the first annual eisteddfod, 27 October 1950.

"Frankie" Williams, a genial resident of Saundersfoot pictured by the anchor salvaged from the Russian schooner *Treviga Riga* which was driven ashore at Morfabychan in 1923.

Saundersfoot United AFC XI pictured at their Broadfield ground in 1948. From left to right, back row: W. Edwards, C. Phelps, T. Williams, Ken Daniels, H. Richards, B. Brown, O. Pulford, J. Phillips, C. Lawrence, G. Phillips, T. Morris, R. Morris, W. Williams, W. Badham. Front row: D. Llewellyn, G. Williams, G. Badham, B. Jenkins, C. Williams (captain), T. Ollin, E. Bateson, N. Greenwood, W. Jones.

The aftermath of the Cambrian Hotel gas explosion, November 1984.

Saundersfoot Cricket Club, 1955. From left to right, back row: Don Fletcher, Gareth Evans, Tony Lomas, Martin Palmer, Frank Williams. Front row: Clifton John, Roy Whitbread, Barry Woods, Colwyn Williams (captain), Billy Scale, David Thomas.

St Issell's Parish Council, Saundersfoot, 1954. From left to right: H. Davies, N. Greenwood, H. Jones, S. Harries, R. Read, P. Larsen, T. Williams, Rt. Hon. Lord Merthyr. A presentation was made to Mr Read to mark his retirement as Saundersfoot's postmaster.

The family of George Williams, 7 Milford Terrace, Saundersfoot, 1919. From left to right, back row: A. Williams, J. Williams, C. Williams, G. King (son-in-law), T. Williams. Middle row: E. Williams, R. Williams (mother), G. Williams (father), N. Williams, F. Williams. Kneeling: K. Williams, S. Williams.

Five

Tenby: High Street, The Norton and Croft, White Lion Street, Warren Street

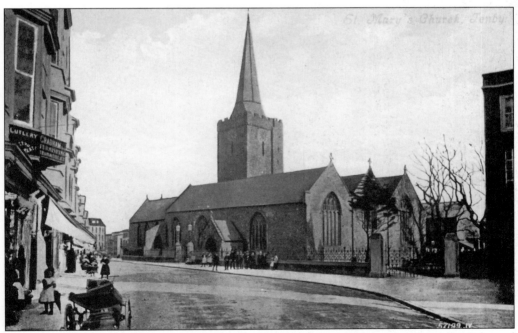

St Mary's Church, High Street, Tenby, *c.* 1902. It was built in the Early English and perpendicular style.

Panoramic view over Tenby from North Cliff, *c.* 1890.

F. F & Co.

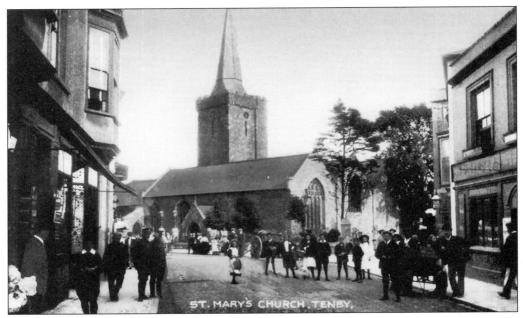

St Mary's Church, High Street, *c.* 1913.

Interior of St Mary's Church, *c.* 1909.

Mr Gunter's boot and shoe shop, *c*. 1910. "Under Gunter's clock" was a well known rendezvous for courting couples.

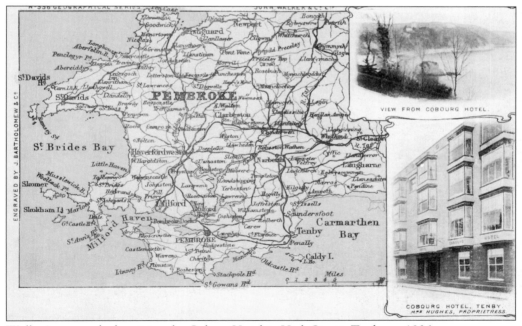

Walker's postcard advertising the Coburg Hotel in High Street, Tenby, *c*. 1906.

High Street, *c.* 1921.

High Street, *c.* 1924.

84

High Street, *c*. 1910.

North Sands viewed from the Peerless Hotel, *c.* 1930.

Tenby harbour as seen from High Street, *c.* 1936.

The Norton, 1912.

The Norton, *c.* 1904.

The Croft, c. 1911.

The White Hart Hotel, c. 1903.

The North Walk, *c.* 1908.

The North Walk to the sands, *c.* 1921.

White Lion Street (formerly called Gate Street), *c.* 1900.

De Valence Gardens, *c.* 1909. These beautiful gardens contained a covered bandstand for first class entertainment and social dances. They were named after William de Valence, Earl of Pembroke.

Interior of the De Valence Pavilion, *c.* 1920.

De Valence Gardens, *c.* 1912.

The Congregational Church, Warren Street, *c.* 1905.

Congregational Church festival day, 27 May 1914.

Congregational Church, *c.* 1901.

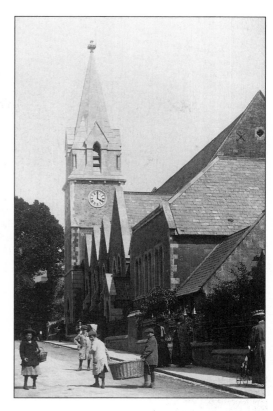

W.H. Smith & Son, newsagent, Warren Street. The first branch of the company in Tenby was opened here on 4 January 1906. The present day premises are situated in High Street.

Tenby railway station, *c*. 1905.

Tenby railway station, *c*. 1947.

94

Six

South Parade, Five Arches, Esplanade

Tenby: "The Naples of Wales."

Climate : Mild and Salubrious.
Population : 4,500.
Distance from London, per G.W.R.,
262 miles.
Unrivalled Sea Bathing.
Picturesque Scenery.
Good Fishing and Boating.
A Town of Ancient Historical Associations.
Fine Golf Links.

Old Gateway and Tower, Tenby.

Postcard advertising Tenby, *c.* 1907.

South Parade, *c.* 1907.

South Parade, *c.* 1904.

War Memorial and town gardens, *c.* 1921.

Entrance to the Five Arches with the Bush Inn on the left, *c.* 1920. Opposite is Evans' grocery shop.

The arches of South Gate viewed from St George's Street, *c.* 1895. Note the private residence on the right pictured here before it became a grocery business. The photograph was taken by Charles Smith Allen, Pembrokeshire's pioneer photographer.

A Charles Smith Allen photograph of the Five Arches and the town wall, *c.* 1895.

Locals pose in St George's Street for Charles Smith Allen, *c*. 1892.

Sutton Street with Tenby Bowling Club on the left, *c.* 1904.

South Cliff Street or Marine Parade, *c.* 1906.

Promenading along the Esplanade, *c.* 1909.

Imperial Hotel situated on the Esplanade, *c.* 1905. It provided its residents with splendid views of the South Sands and Caldey Island, *c.* 1905.

Seven

Tudor Square, South Sands, The Harbour, North Sands

Tudor Square with the Dr Frederick Dyster Memorial in the background. This was erected by the doctor in the 1860s in memory of his friend Colonel Thomas Wedgwood who had fought at Waterloo.

Griffiths' Temperance Hotel, now called Plantagenet House, Quay Hill, *c.* 1908.

The late fifteenth century Tudor merchant's house situated in Bridge Street, *c.* 1903. The building was given to the National Trust by Tenby Council in 1938 and after extensive restoration it is now a tourist attraction.

The Old Arch near the harbour, 1901.

Tenby golf links and the old clubhouse, c. 1909. Formed in September 1888, it is the oldest golf club in Wales.

The sand dunes and marram grass mingle in the area known as the Burrows. St Catherine's Island is visible on the right.

Great Western Railway postcard advertising Tenby as a popular holiday resort, c. 1906.

The official opening of Shanly's Pavilion, 12 July 1929.

Shanly's Pavilion, together with its bandstand, 1929. The Pavilion was a multi-purpose amusement centre consisting of a restaurant, cinema, skating rink, dance hall and roof garden.

Shanly's Pavilion and Tenby golf course, *c*. 1931.

Castle Sands bathing machines with Lexden Terrace in the background, *c*. 1904.

Advertisement card for the Imperial Hotel, *c.* 1922.

South Sands bathing machines on the water's edge advertising Beecham's pills, *c.* 1909. "Worth a guinea a box" these pills saved "doctor's bills" and were reputed to be the "key to health".

The bandstand with St Catherine's Island behind. Large crowds of tourists were attracted to afternoon and evening performances here. It was demolished in 1940 as the metal it contained was required for the war effort. The new Castle Hill bandstand was opened on 31 August 1991.

Bathing machines and St Catherine's Island, *c.* 1907.

The Royal Victoria Pier which had been officially opened in 1899 by the Duchess of York. From here steamer cruises were run by P. & A. Campbell and Pockett's Bristol Channel Steam Packet Co. to Swansea, Ilfracombe, Weston-Super-Mare and Bristol. Regrettably, this pier is no longer in existence having been demolished between 1952 and 1954.

The William and Mary Devey lifeboat on the launching stage, c. 1916 The Tenby lifeboat station crew have a proud record of rescues, often in exceptionally difficult circumstances.

The monument on Castle Hill is the Welsh memorial for the Prince Consort, Albert, husband of Queen Victoria. The Welsh inscription on the pedestal translates as "Albert the Good, Consort of our beloved Queen Victoria, and Dragon of Wales is invincible". It was unveiled by the Duke of Connaught on 2 August 1865.

Tenby harbour, c. 1906.

A Charles Smith Allen photograph of Tenby luggers and smacks moored in the harbour, c. 1890.

The harbour, *c.* 1903.

The old harbour or sluice, *c.* 1929.

Fishermen's cottages by the harbour, *c*. 1903.

St Julian's Fishermen's Chapel, built in 1878.

North Sands, Goscar Rock and Tenby harbour, *c.* 1885. The bathing machines on this beach advertised Pears Soap. This is another photograph taken by Charles Smith Allen.

119

Eight
Tenby's Social History

A large crowd of local people gathered for the 1927 Mayor's Sunday civic service and parade through the streets of Tenby. Margaret Jane Jenkins was installed as the town's First Citizen.

Staff at the Great Western Railway station, Tenby, 1906. The stationmaster was Mr James Bowen.

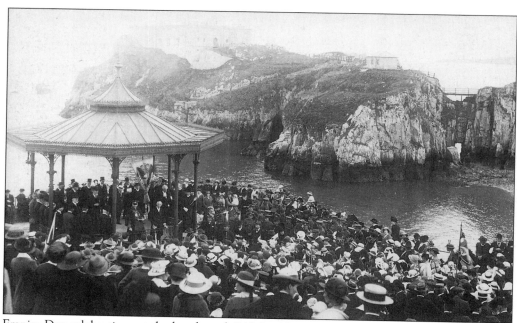

Empire Day celebrations at the bandstand, 24 May 1916.

Procession through the town at the time of King Edward VII's funeral in London, 1910.

Tenby Hunt Week, November 1911, Originally conceived as the Pembrokeshire Hunt Week in the nineteenth century the main focus of the event was Tenby Races, held under National Hunt rules at New Hedges. The last race meeting there took place in 1934.

Mr George Ace in his Bugatti outside Tenby railway station, *c.* 1904. In the early 1890s he opened his Tenby and Pembroke Cycle Company in Warren Street. From cycles the business developed into a flourishing motor agency in Picton Terrace.

The well dressed pupils of St Andrew's private school for boys, North Cliff, 1906.

An important procession wends its way through the High Street, *c.* 1908. St Mary's Church can be seen on the left with the Library reading rooms on the right.

St Margaret's Fair sited on Tom Wall's field, 31 July 1905.

Jack John, the Tenby town crier from 1890 until 1939.

A travelling Llangwm fisherwoman, c. 1911. These women visited Tenby market each week to sell their fish, oysters and prawns.

Lillycrop Fish Merchants boxing fish for despatch by rail to Bristol, Birmingham and London, *c*. 1905. Lillycrop's also had a fishmonger's shop in Lower Frog Street.

Boys Brigade procession from Castle Square, August 1908.

Fishing off the Victoria Pier, *c*. 1905. This was a popular venue for fishing competitions.

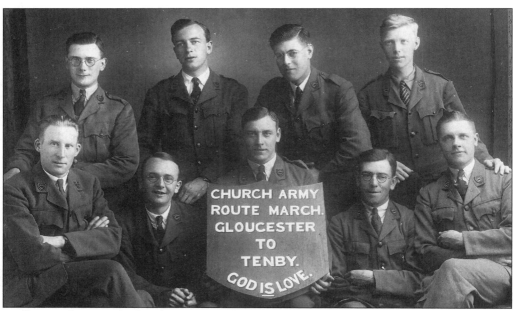

Walkers in the annual Church Army march from Gloucester to Tenby, August 1929.

Jack Hanson (top), lifeboat crew member in the era of cork life jackets and lanterns, *c.* 1884.

Tenby Cymmrodorion Group, 1921

Father, mother and five children with their wooden spades, Tenby beach, 1910.

Picnic on the North Sands, *c.* 1910.

130

A near fatal car accident at the harbour, 1920.

Performance by Gilfach Goch Salvation Army band at the bandstand, *c.* 1908.

Three members of the Tenby Cycling Club, *c.* 1890. This club was formed by George Ace who inspired many cyclists to become active members. Ace, himself, was the road racing cycling champion of Wales from 1879 to 1889. This photograph was taken by Samuel J. Allen, son of Charles Smith Allen.

DE VALENCE PAVILION
TENBY,

⁄ ⁄ ⁄

A GRAND

CONCERT

on

SUNDAY, AUGUST 21ST *1925*

AT 8.15 P.M.

⁄ ⁄ ⁄ ⁄

ARTISTES :

MR. MOSTYN THOMAS

AND THE

LYRIAN SINGERS.

⁄ ⁄ ⁄ ⁄

Conductor : Mr. Richard Williams, L.R.A.M.

Accompanist : Miss. Mary Griffiths.

A Late Trian to Carmarthen and intermediate
stations will leave Tenby at 10.15 p.m.

" Observer " Office, Frog Street, Tenby.

DE VALENCE GARDENS PAVILION, TENBY

Cottage Hospital Concert,

SEPTEMBER 16, 1928.

Programme.

1. (a) Hymn : " Lord of All Being " ....Smith
    (b)   " The Sailors' Chorus " ....Jos. Parry
        THE TENBY MALE OCTETTE.

2. Song ... . " The Lute Player " ....Allitsen
        Mr. MYRDDIN EVANS.

3. Song ...." O Day Divine " ....Oliver
        Miss ANNIE DAVIES.

4. Violin Solo ...." Hre, ji Kati ".....................Hubay
        Mr. WILLIAM JONES.

5. Song ...." Lorena " .... Hughes
        Mr. DAVID HARRY.

6. Song ...." Arise, O Sun " ....Day
        Miss MAGGIE DAVIES.

7. Duet .... " The Voyagers ", ... Sanderson
        Miss ANNIE DAVIES and Mr. MYRDDIN EVANS.

8. Recitation ......" The Sea-King's Burial "..............Mackay
        Miss MIRIAM CHINN.

9.   (a) " Thuringian Volkslied " .... Abt
                (b) " A Catastrophe "....................Sprague
            TENBY MALE OCTETTE.

10. Duet ... ." Where the Chestnuts Bloom " ....Newton
        Misses ANNIE and MAGGIE DAVIES.

11. Song............." The Night Nursery " ....Arundale
        Miss BRONWEN JENKINS.

12. Song... ...." It is Thou"....................... Verdi
        Mr. MYRDDIN EVANS.

13. Song ...." Ring, Bells, Ring " ... .Day
        Miss ANNIE DAVIES.

14. Song................." Sorrow of Death " ....Mendelssohn
        Mr. DAVID HARRY.

15. Violin Solo......" Celebrated Romance " ....Svendsen
        Mr. WILLIAM JONES.

16. Duet......" The Moon hath raised her Lamp " ....
        Messrs. DAVID HARRY and MYRDDIN EVANS.

        " HEN WLAD FY NHADAU "
        " GOD SAVE THE KING."

Accompanist   -   Miss MARY GRIFFITHS

LEACH, " Tenby and County News " Office, Tenby.

De Valence Pavilion,
TENBY.

SATURDAY, 1st JULY, 1933.

A GRAND

Musical Revue

By the Scholars of the

Tenby Council School.

Musical Director :
Mr. RICHARD WILLIAMS, L.R.A.M.

Dances arranged by Miss M. Knowling
and Members of the Staff.

Other items under
Miss G. Mathews, L.R.A.M. & Mr. F. T. Coles.

Costumes made by Parents and Friends,
under the supervision of Mrs. W. Davies.

Stage Effects by Mr W. Noble & Mr Dunkin.

Miss Kate Jones' Orchestra.
Harpist = Mrs. A. J. Newton.   Drums = Mr. C. Rogers.

Accompanists :
Mrs. Wright, Miss M. Griffiths,
Mrs. Carew and Mrs. M. D. Morgan.

Matinee = Doors open at 2.30.   To commence at 3.

Evening :
Doors open at 7.30.   To commence at 8.

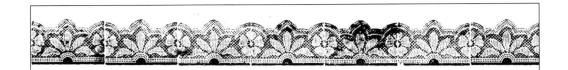

No **4**

"WINGS FOR VICTORY"
CONCERT

SUNDAY, MAY 23rd, 1943.

ROYAL PLAYHOUSE, TENBY

(Kindly given free of charge by Mrs. E. A. Parker).

CONCERT AND PROGRAMME

ARRANGED BY ALBERT BEVAN.

Concert under the auspices of the 1st Batt.
Pembrokeshire Home Guard

(*By Permission of Lieut.-Col. P. R. Howells*).

Special Thanks to Mr. H. E. Weight (Manager of the Royal Playhouse),
Mrs. Basham and Staff for their co-operation.

E. H. Leach, Printer, South Parade, Tenby.

Greenhill Grammar School

TENBY

Headmaster : Mr. G. C. GIBSON, M.Sc., A.R.I.C., J.P.

PROGRAMME

for

THE FESTIVAL OF BRITAIN

OPEN DAY

Wednesday, July 11th, 1951

The Official Opening by
His Worship the Mayor, Councillor W. S. John,
takes place in the Gymnasium at 2.15 p.m.

IMPORTANT NOTE :

It will be observed from the time-table, on the centre page, that some events are taking place simultaneously. Visitors are recommended to consult this time-table to ensure that all the items offered are seen

N.B.—Teas will be served at a charge of one shilling in the A.T.C. Hut in the Boys' Playground, from 4 p.m. onwards

---

Bert Edwards, St. Peter's Road, Milford Haven

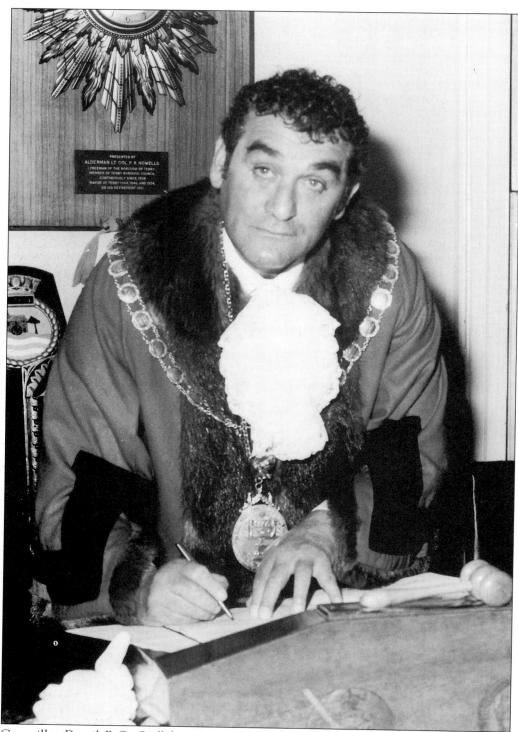

Councillor Denzil R.G. Griffiths, Mayor of Tenby in 1975, 1985, 1986 and 1987. He has represented Tenby and District Council for the past 28 years.

Charles Crockford (engineer) and Alan Thomas (coxswain), two members of the Tenby lifeboat crew.

The present Tenby lifeboat *Sir Galahad*, a steel-hulled 47ft Tyne class self-righting boat. It was launched on 29 September 1986 by HRH Princess Alexandra.

Narcissus pseudo narcissus obvalaris, better known as the Tenby daffodil. This is truly the native daffodil of Wales, the kind that St David would have seen in the countryside. In 1974 the Tenby in Bloom Committee purchased 2,000 Tenby daffodil bulbs which were planted on roadside verges leading into Tenby. It was also selected as a featured flower at the 1992 Garden Festival held in Ebbw Vale.

140

Actor and film director Kenneth Griffiths (centre) made his stage debut in Greenhill School's production of *Richard of Bordeaux* at Super Theatre, Tenby in 1937.

John Thomas was appointed as Tenby's official town crier in June 1981. He is a member of the Ancient and Honourable Guild of Town Criers and has represented Tenby at the British and World Town Criers Championships in the Isle of Wight, Belgium and Canada.

Before John Thomas, Mr Tyssul Jones Thomas (pictured above) held the position of town crier. He was awarded the Military Medal and Bar for acts of bravery in the field while serving with the 7th Battalion of the King's Shropshire Light Infantry during the First World War. He was also an officer of the Order of St John of Jerusalem.

Staff of the *Tenby Observer* and *Narberth Weekly News* at a celebratory dinner at the Royal Gate House Hotel marking the centenary of the *Tenby Observer* (1853–1953). Seated centre with the Mayor (Alderman Howard Hart) are Mr H.G. Walters (editor/proprietor) and Mrs Walters.

Ministers and friends at the 21st anniversary services for the pastorate of Rev Lumley Williams, Deer Park Baptist Church, Tenby, 1953. From left to right, seated: The Mayor of Tenby (Cllr W.S. John), Miss Kate Howells (senior deaconess), Rev J. Lumley Williams (pastor), Mrs J. Lumley Williams, The Mayoress of Tenby (Mrs W.S. John). Behind Rev Lumley Williams is Rev R. Emrys Davies of Swansea who conducted the services.

Tenby and District Primary Schools athletic team, winners at the county primary schools athletic sports in 1952.

Greenhill County School football XI, 1936/37 season. From left to right, back row: Jack Garland, Dennis Griffiths, Billy Griffiths, Douglas Nicholls, Pat Ridley, Stanley Edwards, Garfield Lewis. Seated: Mr J.T. Griffith (headmaster), Arthur Ormond, George Edwards (captain), Dennis Hullah, Mr H.J. Williams (senior master). Front row: Clem John, Ron Brace, Trevor Ford, George Badham.

Greenhill County School football XI, 1946/47 season. From left to right, standing: Bryn Evans, Colwyn Williams, David Williams, Eric John, Brian Morris, Tom Griffiths, Seated: Howell Daniels, the author, Terry Denney (captain), Jeffrey Thomas, Terry Morris. Front: Martin Palmer, Gwyn Llewellyn.

Greenhill County School hockey XI, 1941/42. From left to right, standing: Stella Hooper, Marie Kinmouth, Annie Hodges, Christine Nash, Betsy Lewis, Jean Thomas. Seated: Sylvia Morse. Joyce Hammersley, Peggy Hullah (captain), Mavis Rowlands, Doreen Wright.

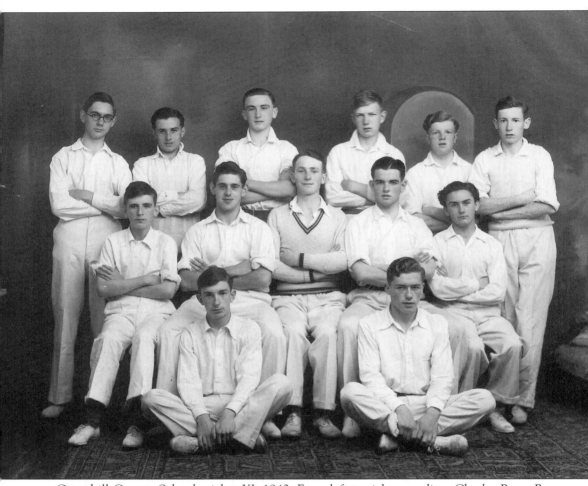

Greenhill County School cricket XI, 1942. From left to right, standing: Charles Burn, Roger Williams, John Ebsworth, John Morgan, Henry Carew, Owen Morse. Seated: Neville Williams, Ronald Walker, Victor Hughes (captain), Peter Hammersley, Alan Rodway. Front: David John, William Thomas.

Tenby Council School rugby XV which swept all before it in winning the Pembrokeshire Shield and Knockout Cup, 1935–36. From left to right, standing: Seth Williams, Peter Diment, Fred Phillips, Arthur Booker, David Gibby, Arthur Ormond, Stanley Phillips, Angelo Fecci. Seated: ? Rixon, Ron Brace, Philip Hearnshaw, Hugh John (captain), Peter Brace, -?-, David Booker. Front: Donald Hullah, Alan John, "Boy Stray" (mascot), Jack Fish, ? Harper.

Billy John's rugby XV, Tenby, 1936/37 season.

The end of a successful season for Tenby United rugby XV, 1932/33.

Mr T.P. Hughes in action on Tenby bowling green, 1929.

Winners of the annual Tenby Bowling Club tournament, 10 August 1957. Gold cup: Llew Edwards, Haverfordwest; Five Arches Cup: Crofton John, Tenby; Silver Bowl: N.(Nat)H. Rees, Dinas Powys.

Crofton John, winner of the Tenby Gold Cup in 1969.

Hayden Guy, Winner of the Tenby Gold Cup in 1979.

The 1928 winner is presented with the Gold Cup by Lady Hughes-Morgan, wife of the President of Tenby Bowling Club, Sir David Hughes-Morgan.

Winners of the annual Tenby Bowling Club tournament, 1983. From left to right: The Mayor, Cllr Wilf Hardy MBE, The Lady Mayoress, Mrs Christine Hardy, Silver Bowl winner, Malcolm Bishop, Gold Cup winner, John Nicholl, Five Arches Cup winner, Les Davies, Dr Evan Williams.

Tenby Bowling Club President, R.F. (Bobby) Diment, 1985.

Simon Evans of Saundersfoot, winner of both the Gold Cup and the Silver Bowl in 1985.

Tudor Square and St Mary's Church, Tenby, c. 1930.

Acknowledgements

I wish to record with grateful thanks the generous assistance given to me by many people during the preparation of this book. Their names include: Mrs N. Davies, Mrs A. Morris, Mrs P. Griffiths, Cllr Mrs R. Hayes, J.P., Lens of Sutton, Mr B. Lewis, Mr C. Cox, Mr A. Parcell, Mr W. Burgess, Mr C. Williams, Cllr A. Lawrence, Mr F. Williams, Mr Neil Dickenson, Mr A. Ormond MBE, Mr J. Thomas, Mr W. Hardy MBE, the staff of both Tenby Museum and Tenby Library, Simon Eckley (Wales editor for Chalford Publishing).

This list could not be completed without mention of Mr David Buxton, Senior Editor at Chalford Publishing. Our meeting earlier this year at the York postcard fair provided the spark which has led to the publication of this book.